KV-682-906

Public Interest
New Models for Delivering Public Services?

Public Interest

New Models for Delivering Public Services?

**Jane Steele, Mary Tetlow
and Alison Graham**
Public Management Foundation

CALOUSTE GULBENKIAN FOUNDATION, LONDON

Published by
Calouste Gulbenkian Foundation
United Kingdom Branch
98 Portland Place
London W1B 1ET
Tel: 020 7908 7604
info@gulbenkian.org.uk
www.gulbenkian.org.uk

© 2003 Calouste Gulbenkian Foundation
    and Public Management Foundation

Public Management Foundation
165 Gray's Inn Road
London WC1X 8UE
Tel: 020 7239 7800

All rights reserved; unauthorised reproduction
of any part of this work in any medium
is strictly prohibited.

The views expressed in this book are those
of the authors, not necessarily those of the
Calouste Gulbenkian Foundation.

ISBN 0 903319 99 3

British Library Cataloguing-in-Publication Data
A catalogue record for this book is available
from the British Library.

Designed by Onvisual, www.onvisual.com
Cover illustration by Sima Vaziry
Printed by Expression Printers Ltd, IP23 8HH

Distributed by Central Books Ltd,
99 Wallis Road, London E9 5LN
Tel: 0845 458 9911, Fax: 0845 458 9912
orders@centralbooks.com
www.centralbooks.co.uk

Contents

Acknowledgements

This study would not have been possible without the many people who agreed to be interviewed. We thank them for being so generous with their time and expertise.

The Public Management Foundation is very grateful to the Calouste Gulbenkian Foundation for funding this study.

Foreword

The debate about the need for new organisational forms for public services, social enterprise and 'not-for-profit' activity shows no sign of abating. Many think tanks, commentators and journalists are developing ideas about new organisational forms, their design and their potential, adding to what has become a wide-ranging discussion that is attracting the attention of a diverse group of institutions and professions.

The possibility of new forms that offer an alternative to traditional public- and private-sector organisations also seems to have appealed to the Government, which has announced new arrangements for railway infrastructure (Network Rail) and for high-performance NHS trusts (Foundation Hospitals). A review of the legislative and regulatory framework for the voluntary sector by the Government's Strategy Unit came out in favour of a new organisational form, the Community Interest Company, to encourage social enterprise.

The Public Management Foundation helped to stimulate this debate in 2001 with our 'idea in progress' about a new organisational form for public services, the Public Interest Company. As discussions developed and innovations were proposed, we decided to take another look at the issues, but this time from the other end of the telescope. Instead of starting with proposals for a new type of organisation, we set out to explore the problems that public services face while working with their current forms of organisation. By involving people who have the most immediate experience of the practical difficulties encountered in delivering effective services, that is, those who work in delivery organisations, as well as policy-makers and advisers, we set out to ground our next contribution to the debate firmly in the reality of everyday service delivery.

With the financial support of the Calouste Gulbenkian Foundation, we invited a wide range of people to discuss whether there is a real need for new organisational forms in public services. Not surprisingly, most people involved in the day-to-day delivery of public services are not focused on the possibility of a future organisational form. However, they are very concerned about the difficulties of their current organisations in delivering effective services. There was a considerable degree of consensus about the nature of these problems, which their experience showed to be interconnected in complex ways. Further discussion and analysis indicated that these problems are related to the structural features of their organisations, and to the wider political and public service environments in which they operate.

These complex interconnections made two important messages clear to us: first, there is merit in developing and testing new forms of organisation for public services, but, second, any new forms that are developed must address, in an integrated fashion, the interconnectedness of the problems facing public service organisations. To pick and choose features of organisational forms that seem to address those individual problems that are most prominent to the media and politicians at any particular time is unlikely to be successful.

What is needed now is rigorous learning from experiment and experience. This important debate is much in need of an empirical base. The issues are too abstract, too complex, and too important to take further while understanding is limited by the constraints of existing forms, and ideas about new and better ways of serving the public remain untested.

Greg Parston
Chairman, Public Management Foundation

1. Introduction

The intention of this study is to look a little more deeply into the debate about organisational form and public service delivery. What are the problems that practitioners and commentators find with current modes of delivery? How do these problems manifest themselves? Are new organisational forms the answer? In preparing this publication we interviewed a cross-section of leading thinkers and practitioners in search of answers to these questions. We asked them to consider the relationship between public services and the organisational form used to deliver them, and to consider how new forms should be governed and made accountable and efficient.

The Public Management Foundation has for some time been concerned with the case for a new organisational form that we have called 'the Public Interest Company'.[1] Our earlier publications set out 'ideas in progress' about a new organisational form to deliver public services, a form that might build on the advantages of forms that are characteristic of the public, voluntary and private sectors, while avoiding the pitfalls that each has for the delivery of public services.

Since our earlier publications there has been considerable interest in the use of alternative organisational forms for public services. Ministers have used the term 'Public Interest Company' in connection with the management of the railway system and with Foundation Hospitals, but without defining an organisational form for such an entity. A concept with many similar characteristics to the Public Interest Company (called the 'Community Interest Company') has been recommended in the Cabinet Office Strategy Unit review of the voluntary sector.[2]

This project

This project set out to explore the views of practitioners and policy-makers in public services on the following three questions:

- What are the problems encountered in attempts to deliver high-quality and effective public services?

---

1. *An Idea in Progress: The case for the Public Interest Company, a new form of enterprise for public service delivery* (London, Public Management Foundation, 2001); and Charles Brecher, *The Public Interest Company as a Mechanism to Improve Service Delivery: Suggestions for the reorganization of the London Underground and National Health Service trusts* (London, Public Management Foundation, 2002).
2. *Private Action, Public Benefit: A review of charities and the wider not-for-profit sector* (London, Strategy Unit, Cabinet Office, 2002).

- How are these problems related to the forms of organisation used to deliver public services?
- What features would alternative organisational forms need in order to be effective in public services?

The study was carried out in two main phases. The first involved in-depth, confidential interviews with 18 people: service providers, financiers, policy-makers, regulators, representatives of user and staff interests, researchers and commentators. Interviewees included leading thinkers in the management of public service, drawn from research and practitioner backgrounds, from the private, public and voluntary sectors and from trade unions. We also interviewed people already involved in the debate about new organisational forms – in general and in specific sectors.

We asked questions about current perceived problems with public services, and about features which new organisational forms might need to possess to address these problems. Questions covered such areas as governance and accountability, financing, the necessity for competition and different approaches to motivation.

The second phase of the project explored the same research questions in three specific service areas that receive public funding – support services to schools, social housing, and residential care for elderly people. These areas are currently served by different types of organisation, including some outside the public sector, and were chosen to provide not only a diversity of current approaches but also a range of social needs and user groups; different systems of regulation, governance and accountability; and different funding requirements and arrangements. In each area we interviewed between seven and nine people, giving us a sector-specific cross-section of the perspectives outlined above for phase one.

During the project we also organised two seminars for practitioners and policy-makers in the field (see Appendix). At the first, Nick Timmins, Public Policy Editor of the *Financial Times*, and Professor Julian Le Grand of the London School of Economics discussed whether the idea of alternative organisational forms for public services was 'an imaginative solution or a red herring'. At the second, Professor Gerry Stoker of the University of Manchester considered the need to make organisations delivering public services accountable to the public. The presentations and debates at both seminars informed both the ongoing thinking about the use of alternative organisational forms and the discussion presented here.

A topical debate

There is clearly widespread interest in developing organisational forms that reflect the special needs of public services. It is fair to say that this debate has so far provided more questions than answers. The demise of Railtrack caused considerable discussion about the potential conflict between public and shareholder interest in public service delivery. Proposals for Foundation Hospitals have focused attention on the desirability of distance from direct government involvement in the day-to-day management of services and on the need to find private means of raising capital for public-sector projects. They have also generated discussion about what happens when what is perceived as an essential public service, but is outside direct government control, fails financially.

At the same time a government review of the legal and regulatory framework of charities and the wider not-for-profit sector has further raised the profile of issues about organisational form. The review recommends reform of the legal framework for organisational forms and in particular the creation of a Community Interest Company form to meet the needs of social enterprise. Its characteristics are:

- 'Protection of assets against distribution to members or shareholders;
- Ability to choose the limited by guarantee or by shares format, with full adherence to UK and European company law and guidelines, including rules on insolvency, accountancy, and governance;
- Ability to issue preference shares with a fixed rate of return (this applies to both the limited by guarantee and limited by shares models);
- Increased requirements in terms of transparency and accountability;
- A requirement to have a clause in the constitution setting out the objects of the company;
- A check at the point of registration that the objects of the organisation are in the public and community interest, with subsequent changes being subject to regulatory approval.'[3]

This form is designed to address the particular requirements of organisations that wish to develop social enterprise, but find current options for legal form too restrictive. However, the underlying principles may have wider application to larger institutions and organisations providing public services. Indeed, the proposed model has much in common with our own earlier proposals for a Public Interest Company.[4] This will surely raise questions about whether there is a fundamental difference between the forms required for the types of public interest activity currently delivered by the existing voluntary sector and larger-scale institutions like railways and hospitals. The alternative might be a single new organisational form to address the requirements of a wide range of public functions.

---

3. See footnote 2 on page 7 (p. 54).
4. See footnote 1 on page 7.

Why now? Background to the current discussion about new organisational forms for delivery of public services

In the past, the argument has focused on whether the private sector is a suitable vehicle for the delivery of public services. Widespread contracting and privatisation have given plenty of examples of how this can be done. The controversies, however, do not go away. Debates continue about whether the private sector can be 'trusted', whether there is a conflict between commitment to public service and profit motive, and how democratic bodies can retain control over the quality of services that are delivered.

The other side of the argument – that the public sector is inefficient, monolithic and unresponsive, however much it is reformed or modernised – also continues. Over a long period, the general drive to improve public services has focused on perceived inefficiencies and low standards in public-sector delivery, especially in the NHS. At the same time there has been considerable growth in the delivery of public services by voluntary bodies, commissioned or grant-aided by the statutory sector. The result is a complex mosaic of provision.

Much of this increased use of the private and voluntary sectors has been in response to specific issues – such as the need to raise capital outside the Public Sector Borrowing Requirement – and to specific policy initiatives designed to break the public-sector monopoly, such as Compulsory Competitive Tendering. At the same time, there has been considerable disquiet about failures. Railtrack and British Energy are examples of high-profile problems in erstwhile public-sector bodies transferred to the private sector. The arguments about the strengths and weaknesses of different approaches depend at least in part on the political ideologies of those who propose them, and are therefore unlikely to be resolved easily.

There is little consensus on whether the answer lies in experimenting with new organisational forms. Advocates of the need for such forms demonstrate the drawbacks of the traditional public-sector model and at the same time point out that private- and voluntary-sector models were not designed for public service delivery and therefore also have disadvantages. Proposals for an entirely new form, the Public Interest Company model, or for the adaptation of existing mutuals (Industrial and Provident Societies) call for a purpose-designed form that incorporates the best of all existing options and avoids their drawbacks. The problem lies in agreeing what the drawbacks are and in reaching a consensus about the features that would be required of a new organisational form. It is also difficult to envisage the sort of policy environment that would be required for a new organisational form to flourish.

This project set out to explore whether there is a real, felt need for a new organisational form in public service, or whether this is a solution in search of a problem. Our interviews revealed considerable interest in the issues within the practitioner and policy community, but people readily acknowledged that they find the issues complicated and hard to understand.

The difficulties experienced by interviewees in addressing these questions were due in part to unfamiliarity with the concepts and ways of thinking, and in part to the inherent complexities of the issues. People found it quite difficult to separate thinking about organisational forms from the immediate policy and political environment in which they work. This hampered investigation of some of the themes of our project.

It must also be recognised that the issues discussed here have a political dimension. Inevitably, a number of the people we interviewed had views that were based on personal political beliefs or positions. For example, some clearly felt that the only delivery alternative to the public sector was the private sector; while for others the retention of public service under direct control of elected representatives was the overriding concern. These positions were based on ideological viewpoints and experiences of privatisation in the past. It has sometimes been difficult, therefore, to separate issues related to organisational form from these wider concerns.

2. Problems and potential solutions

Interviewees for this project were either concerned with service delivery or with thinking about the means of delivery. There was no consensus on whether new forms are needed and no great demand for them amongst practitioners. Nor was there agreement about other ways of reforming public service delivery. Our informants' difficulties, as they readily admitted, came in tracing the connections between problems and organisational form, and in separating the influences of organisational form, policy environment and politics on delivery. This does not necessarily mean, however, that there is no scope for a new organisational form that public services might test and to which existing institutions could migrate.

In this chapter we consider our interviewees' views of the following:

- What problems are encountered in delivering public services through existing forms? Could alternative organisational forms help to address these problems?
- What features would alternative forms need in order to be effective?
- What sort of environment is needed for alternative forms to deliver?

The chapter concludes with a suggested approach for assessing the suitability of organisational forms for the delivery of public services.

2.1. What problems are encountered in delivering high-quality, effective public services through existing organisational forms? Could alternative organisational forms help to address these problems?

Our interviewees identified the following areas of concern:

- the need for organisational autonomy;
- lack of capacity to attract high-calibre managers;
- difficulties in being accountable to service users and the public;
- organisations that are too large to be effective;
- access to capital;
- the need for incentives to improve services;
- difficulties in creating partnership working between organisations;
- mixed experience of service delivery by the private sector;
- the need for a plurality of providers.

There was little consensus on the relative importance of these factors, apart from widespread agreement about the constraining effects of the lack of organisational autonomy.

The need for organisational autonomy

The need for greater autonomy for public service organisations was seen as the most serious problem, from which others flowed. However, it was hard for people to imagine how greater autonomy could actually be achieved. Their thinking was heavily influenced by the policies of the current government and traditions in the British public sector. Those who make decisions about the way services are delivered feel constrained by a strongly centralised service delivery culture in the public sector.

Centralisation sets a pattern that runs throughout the public service delivery machinery. At all levels, public service delivery is seen as heavily hierarchical and 'top-down'. The capacity to get messages back from the bottom upwards – from direct contact with users – is poor. This pattern has existed for many years and is culturally ingrained. Increased central control over the past 20 years has reinforced and in many cases exacerbated it, but a tendency to hierarchy and lack of creativity is inherent in public service delivery in the UK. This tendency is not merely a product of the current Labour Government and its modernising agenda but is seen as having been established over a long period.

Central government exercises a high degree of control over local services by setting standards, monitoring plans, inspecting delivery and regulating investment. Where there have been attempts to encourage autonomy for local public service organisations, and a creative and responsive approach to service provision (such as the creation of NHS trusts in the 1990s) government departments are felt to have had problems 'letting go'.

Thus, while a new organisational form could certainly offer greater autonomy, the issue of autonomy is perceived not just as one of organisational form but as one of political and organisational culture. Public services are central to government policy, and government, through the machinery of Whitehall and the regulatory agencies, exercises a high degree of control over their delivery. The modernisation agenda of the present Government has in many ways exacerbated this situation by driving the reform process from the centre, in an attempt to maximise its impact.

The limits on organisational autonomy are felt to be strongly related to some of the problems that are currently inherent to public service, including the calibre of management, the capacity of public services to respond to local needs, and the capacity to be creative in delivery. Many feel that the public sector has become monolithic and unresponsive, that modernisation has had little effect on the 'front line' of service delivery. Restrictions on autonomy mean that the people who make decisions that affect services are not necessarily close to the results of those decisions, and this reduces their effectiveness. There appears to be tension between a general desire to overcome the disadvantages of centralisation by encouraging local autonomy and a simultaneous desire for equality of standards in service provision. Inevitably, local autonomy is likely to produce diversity of provision and with it some inequalities in standards. There seems to be no consensus about whether this inevitable variation in standard of service is acceptable.

Lack of capacity to attract high-calibre managers

Managers in the public sector are not seen as exercising a high degree of creativity – perhaps because they are constrained by their lack of autonomy. This is perceived by many people to be a fundamental problem with the present situation. There is little incentive to go into public service if you are a motivated, creative potential senior manager. Perhaps alternative ways of doing things – new organisational forms – might be a way of attracting people who are otherwise deterred from entering public service management. Views on this point diverged – some interviewees apparently believed that more autonomy would of itself encourage existing managers to be more creative regardless of organisational form, while others felt that management practice can be invigorated only by introducing 'new blood', or by radical organisational change including change of form.

Difficulties in being accountable to service users and the public

Governance of most public service organisations is rooted in the democratic and electoral systems of the UK. For example, services provided by local authorities are controlled, ultimately, by councillors who are elected locally. People running health and police services have lines of accountability running up to ministers in central government. Many people working in public services see these structures of accountability as remote from and unresponsive to local needs, although some make considerable efforts to involve service users and the local community in decision-making about services, and are seeking approaches that could help them to do this more effectively.

By giving public service responsibilities to bodies using new organisational forms it would be possible to deliver services through entities that were smaller and more focused than many of the large public bodies currently in operation. These could more easily develop effective dialogues with users and stakeholders, and new forms also allow the possibility of new governance structures, including stakeholder and user representation on the board, and thus more control by users.

However, new organisations delivering public services are likely to receive income from government as well as or instead of directly from users. For this reason, there also need to be ways within democratic structures to ensure accountability for the use of public money, and to allow government-led reform of a public service as a whole, in response to changing needs at national level. Some people argue that the distinction between public accountability and overbearing government control is a fine one, to be found only in the eye of the beholder.

Organisations that are too large to be effective
There is a perception of public service organisations as large and inflexible, incapable of responding quickly to changing needs, and a widespread concern that this breeds inefficiency, inertia or resistance to change. The process of change is slow and expensive. If new forms allow the creation of smaller bodies, perhaps with a single service focus, these might be better able to adapt to changing situations and to concentrate on the essentials of high-quality delivery and on achieving improvements in their particular area without being distracted by too wide a remit.

Access to capital
Many current examples of former public services now being delivered by the private sector were initiated, to a very large extent, to take advantage of opportunities to attract private capital. The 'annual spending round mentality' and stringent rules about borrowing in the public sector are often blamed for problems with capital investment. Alternative ways of raising capital for major projects using the Private Finance Initiative (PFI) and public–private partnerships are now widespread. Many see this as a direct result of a reduction in funding for public services over the years. Typically, capital investment has been neglected and when situations become critical and require major funding, the private sector is the only available source. However, current mechanisms, like PFI, are often criticised as uneconomic.

The opportunity to raise capital and to reinvest surplus in the service is attractive. New forms of organisation would be able to take advantage of this opportunity if they had powers to raise finance and if borrowing decisions were based on their financial viability and the willingness of private-sector finance to get involved, rather than being influenced by government management of public expenditure. Such access to capital would allow organisations to take a longer-term view of financial planning than is currently possible. The implications of this for more creative thinking are also seen as appealing.

The need for incentives to improve services
Monolithic structures with no competition tend to be inefficient and conservative. In the public sector, there are few incentives, either for individuals or organisations, to improve quality, to innovate or to develop

entrepreneurial approaches. Attempts to create markets where there is a monopoly supplier are problematic; there needs to be real choice and real risk if competition is to be a spur to improvement.

There are alternative incentives for improvement, including target-setting and regulation. In such cases, much depends on the degree of 'cosiness' in the relationship between the target-setter and inspector and the service delivery organisation. These mechanisms are widely in use, but are seen as the machinery of centralisation, which may encourage efficiency but which stifles creativity. Further, if these mechanisms are reduced or withdrawn, there is a risk that, in a non-competitive environment, there will be little incentive to improve.

Difficulties in creating partnership working between organisations

While there is widespread recognition that many of the social problems with which public service organisations are attempting to deal (such as social exclusion, poor health and unemployment) require the co-ordinated efforts of a number of organisations, such partnership working is difficult to achieve in practice. Research into partnership working reveals much good will but frequent difficulties in achieving a clear shared vision which fits well with the objectives and working practices of all parties.[5]

There is a risk that moves to increase organisational autonomy and independence might further inhibit partnership working, if organisations were not tied into public-sector directives to co-operate. However, greater autonomy could free organisations from incompatible targets and funding rules, thus making partnership a more practical possibility.

Mixed experience of service delivery by the private sector

Experience of the involvement of the private sector in public service delivery has been varied. Here, the relationship between organisational form, purpose and culture comes to the fore. The primary function of a public service organisation is to deliver that service. In theory, it can adapt and change as needs arise over time. In contrast, private-sector organisations are generally perceived as having profit as their primary motive, and there is concern amongst people in the public sector about the possibility of conflict between this and public service values. There are examples of efficiency gains resulting from the involvement of small companies (usually companies limited by guarantee) in aspects of local public service delivery. However, the conflict between public and shareholder interest in Public Limited Companies (PLCs), which was most famously evident in the demise of Railtrack, is widely felt to be a serious danger to public service delivery.

---

5 *Developing Productive Partnerships: A bulletin* (London, District Audit, Audit Commission, October 2002).

Problems with the involvement of the private sector have sometimes been the result of inefficient contracting and purchasing practice by the public sector, leading to poorly specified services. There is also concern about protection for public service employees when their jobs are transferred to private-sector organisations which may not maintain terms and conditions in the long term. This concern is reinforced where new staff are employed with less favourable terms and conditions, raising fears about the quality of staff as well as about employment protection. However, these issues are now being addressed through a draft code of practice. On the positive side, private-sector organisations are sometimes seen as being successful in branding and badging their service delivery in ways that can be appealing to users.

The creation of a new type of organisation that is clearly identified as non-profit-distributing could help to create public and workforce trust in the form, and to address the anxiety about the transfer of public-sector activity outside the sector. To secure public confidence, assets would need to be protected in the public interest. However, there needs to be flexibility in the system to allow organisations to use assets in appropriate ways to meet their public service objectives.

The need for a plurality of providers

Greater diversity in any sector currently dominated by traditional public-sector provision could be advantageous. A mosaic of different organisations, using different organisational forms, would enable more creative and entrepreneurial approaches to flourish. But the political and policy environment would need to adapt to a trading relationship with providers, and to relinquish some of the command and control structures currently in use. Some people also argue that trade alone will not lead to creativity and efficiency and that competition is also required. Plurality of forms and diversity of providers might, in turn, attract high-quality professionals to work in public service organisations.

Summary

Interviewees identified a number of problems that inhibit the delivery of effective public services. The central theme was the restrictions on the autonomy or freedom of local public service organisations. These constraints are thought to contribute to a greater or lesser extent to most, if not all, of the other difficulties.

There was a range of views about whether new organisational forms could provide a way of addressing these problems. In general, interviewees found it hard to conceptualise how alternative forms might operate in practice. However, some of their difficulties were due to their awareness of the complex ways in which different problems affect one another. Some interviewees felt strongly that a wide range of organisational forms was already available, but that these were poorly understood and could be used more effectively. Others thought that there was potential in alternative forms, and that current models did not provide adequate answers.

It was recognised that many problems have their roots in organisational and public service culture, individual behaviour and people's motivations and values. While a new organisational form might help to shape these, it is not the only or necessarily the most effective way of influencing behaviour. Some interviewees felt that many of these problems could be addressed within present structures, given willingness on the part of politicians, policy-makers and senior executives to grant more autonomy to individual institutions. Thus there was no real consensus that new forms are necessary, though there was widespread interest in the opportunities they might offer to address current problems.

2.2 What features would alternative organisational forms need in order to be effective?

Here we turn to a more detailed discussion of the features that alternative organisational forms are thought to require if they are to succeed in delivering effective services. In many cases people struggled to imagine an organisational form that could readily deliver the advantages associated with greater autonomy, especially in the current public services climate, while protecting the public interest.

There are two main areas that require development:

- accountability and governance;
- motivation and incentives, including issues related to failing organisations and to competition between organisations.

Accountability and governance

It is necessary to develop structures that capitalise on the benefits of greater autonomy – creativity, responsiveness to local needs and so on – while protecting the public's interest in public service design and delivery in services not delivered through the public sector. 'Handing over' public money, in the form of commissioning services, to bodies that are apparently not directly accountable through electoral or public appointment systems is seen to be problematic.

Ways of resolving this dilemma seem more elusive because of a political environment in which government has made the quality of public services a core part of its mission. Many people observe that central government has created a public expectation that it will take responsibility for both success and failure at local level, and that it will therefore be reluctant to relinquish mechanisms of direct control, however ineffective these may be in practice.

For many people the accountability of alternative organisational forms seems difficult to imagine, for three main reasons. First, existing models, and the experience of Compulsory Competitive Tendering and Best Value, often rely on the rigour of the contract to protect the public interest. The business of the delivery organisation is delivering to the contract specifications, and accountability lies with the contracting entity, the local authority or other democratically accountable institution.

Second, a rigorous performance framework that comes with the contracting or commissioning process may give a public body some control over the type and quality of services that are delivered by another organisation but, arguably, removes the benefits of greater autonomy, especially if, as is sometimes the case, the means of achieving outcomes is specified in the framework as well as the outcomes themselves.

A third issue is that a reliance on contracts and performance frameworks may not require the supplier to consult users directly. Most people agree that delivery should be influenced by users' views, and that these views can change over time. Non-public-sector entities probably require means to ensure that the design of their services is directly responsive to user requirements. The market for public services does not mirror the competitive market in the private sector, as the user is not the purchaser of services. Thus the normal mechanism of competition cannot ensure an adequate voice for the user.

The debate about approaches for achieving, first, user-responsiveness and, second, accountability is sometimes confused. There is concern that organisations, in order to be both accountable and user-responsive, might find themselves with boards representing multiple stakeholder interests. Some people feel that such boards are the only means of ensuring that the public interest is properly represented. Others fear that they could stifle the capacity for innovation and become incapable of resolving difficult issues – particularly when political agendas run counter to the experience of those directly involved in service delivery. There is a strong argument for a smaller, executive board that would be separate from the structures and processes required for stakeholder engagement.

There is also a need to develop the role of regulators to make sure that new forms of organisation are accountable both for standards of service and for financial viability. This is an issue to which we return in the investigations of three specific sectors and in our conclusions to this report.

Motivation and incentives

There is a debate about how to put in place the incentives that will motivate both people and organisations to achieve more for the public interest. This debate is concerned partly with the role of competition. Although competition is the means by which the private sector is motivated to improve, this may not be possible for some public services where it is often difficult to create a true market. Monopoly provision is often the *de facto* situation in public services and is inevitable in many areas, for example rural education.

However, in some fields competition has arisen as a result of Compulsory Competitive Tendering for services (waste disposal and rubbish collection, for example) and this could develop further in the future. Large companies have sometimes driven out smaller ones – a market of sorts has arisen, but with increasing control of delivery by non-locally based large private companies.

For some people, competition feels counter to the ethos of partnership, especially for organisations that regard themselves as 'not-for-profit'. As contracting becomes more widespread, many organisations find their ethos has to change in order to respond to an increasingly competitive environment. A new entrepreneurial mindset is developing in some sectors, such as transport. The NHS may continue this trend, if large and successful Foundation Hospitals are encouraged to take over the management of their underperforming neighbours.

Some argue that a true not-for-profit operation is not viable in a competitive environment – that entrepreneurialism and the lack of a profit motive are incompatible. This highlights differences in understanding as to the meaning of 'not-for-profit'. Some argue that charitable intent is not compatible with surplus generation in any circumstances, and thus that not-for-profit means that surpluses are not generated. This is the traditional view. Others recognise a distinction between surplus generation for reinvestment in the service on the one hand and for dividend distribution to shareholders on the other, seeing the former as legitimate not-for-profit activity. This confusion is widespread and may constitute a strong argument against the use of the term 'not-for-profit' and for the use of 'non-profit-distributing' to describe organisations that seek to generate a surplus for reinvestment in their services.

Issues of competition are linked to the question of whether entities charged with delivering public services can fail. Does the increased autonomy associated with a new organisational form bring with it the freedom to fail financially? For most people, the possibility of such an organisation going out of business is unpalatable, if not actually unacceptable, especially in the case of core public services, such as hospitals. However, at the same time, an explicit or implicit acceptance that government will act to prevent such an occurrence is seen as undermining the advantages of autonomy and the incentives to improve performance and efficiency.

Some interviewees expressed a view that, where competition is not present as a major incentive and where there is no, or little, risk of failure, regulation and inspection are crucial as motivators for improvement. Government regulation should encompass both quality standards and financial sustainability. However, people find it very difficult to envisage a regulatory regime that can effectively balance risk management and protection of the public interest against the advantages of autonomy and responsiveness to local needs.

Summary
Just as interviewees sometimes found it difficult to envisage ways in which alternative forms could provide solutions to some of the problems currently perceived in public services, they also found it hard to identify the kinds of features which alternative forms might need. Issues of accountability and user-responsiveness were of crucial concern, and the implications of the potential for failure were particularly difficult to resolve.

2.3 What sort of environment is needed for alternative forms to deliver?
Organisations do not exist in isolation, and many interviewees referred to the kinds of environment needed for success. Key themes were commissioning and procurement, regulation and the encouragement of diversity.

Commissioning and procuring services
The commissioning and procurement of services will form one of the main relationships between the democratically accountable spenders of public money and the organisations who are paid to provide the services. At present, there is a strong sense that the public sector is bad at commissioning and procuring services. Service level agreements run the risk of specifying quantity rather than quality of delivery. Issues may be different where there is a market through which users can express choice directly through purchase – for example in the provision of leisure services. But where the purchaser is exclusively the state on behalf of the user (for example in the NHS) there are concerns that the user has, for all practical purposes, little or no direct voice and that procurement skills are inadequate to the task of developing purchaser/provider agreements that deliver services users expect. Unless the accountability structures of the non-public entities are strengthened, there is a risk that services will not be properly responsive to user requirements.

Regulation in the public interest
Regulation is an additional means of ensuring accountability and of providing an incentive for improvement. It covers two aspects of an entity's functioning – the operational and the financial. Some see a need for these two to be separated. The operational aspect requires regulation through mechanisms similar to current public service means. However, financial regulation – needed to ensure that not-for-profit entities are soundly managed and

unlikely to fail, and to supervise issues like the remuneration of chief executives – requires its own mechanism.

This issue is probably the least clear of all in the current debate on new organisational forms.

Encouraging diversity

The complexities of the relationship between organisational form and function led many people to call for the encouragement of diversity. A range of organisational forms working alongside each other would enable organisations to learn from one another about the suitability of different approaches for meeting different needs. The very existence of contrast and difference could facilitate improvement and development in the quality of services.

Summary

This area was probably the one which interviewees found most difficult to conceptualise. If alternative forms are to take responsibility for service delivery then the regulatory and governance environment in which they operate needs to protect the public interest effectively. This means that appropriate operational and financial regulation should be in place.

2.4 Conclusion: how should we assess the suitability of organisational forms for delivering public services?

There was no consensus among interviewees about the need for new organisational forms for public service delivery. Although there was considerable agreement about the problems that contribute to the difficulties of delivering effective and high-quality services, there was no clear or shared analysis of the connections between these and organisational form. However, there was definite agreement about the problems we currently face in public service delivery, and these problems (described above) are precisely those which advocates of new organisational forms (Public Interest Companies, Community Interest Companies, a stronger role for Mutual organisations) cite as reasons for their positions.

In order to inform this debate further, we developed an analytical framework for assessing the effectiveness of the current structures of some public services, recognising that while structure is not necessarily the entire answer to the problems people encounter, it should contribute to the effectiveness of services and certainly should not impede them.

The following questions would appear to be central to understanding the suitability of organisational forms, and the environment in which they operate, for the provision of public services.

1. **Independence from government and political control:** How much autonomy do organisations have?
2. **Public purpose:** To what extent can the public purpose of the service offered be assured? Can the board or management of the organisation change its purpose without protection of the public's interest?
3. **Non-profit-distributing organisations (NPDOs):** There is widespread concern that private profit could be made from public services. To what extent is this occurring?
4. **Preserving assets for the public interest:** Who owns the assets of public services?
5. **Use and disposal of assets:** How can assets used in public service be disposed of? How would this impact on the public interest?
6. **Public confidence:** Are members of the public confident that the service is committed to the public interest and of appropriate quality and cost – and how have they reacted where alternative forms have been introduced?
7. **Governance and accountability:** Who is responsible for the direction and probity of the organisation, and through what mechanisms is accountability to users ensured?
8. **Finance:** How is capital raised?
9. **Protection for users:** What mechanisms exist to protect individual users who are not direct purchasers of the service?
10. **Efficiency, innovation and enterprise:** How efficient is the organisation? How is efficiency achieved? What incentives are there for innovation and entrepreneurialism?

48572 020000 0485

3. Specific sectors – an introduction

The next phase of this study set out to shed further light on the relationship between organisational forms and service effectiveness by examining in some detail existing provision in three areas: support services to schools, social housing and residential care for the elderly. We set out to ascertain how current provision operates and how those involved in service provision and commissioning view the present situation.

The purpose and history of these three sectors are markedly different. While they all involve organisations outside the public sector in delivering services to the public, they differ from one another in the organisational forms they use.

- Support services to schools are provided mainly by local education authorities. The use of alternative organisational forms in this case is relatively recent, small-scale and still experimental, and our investigations focused on these experiments.
- Provision of social housing by Registered Social Landlords, which take a variety of not-for-profit organisational forms, is now well established and has its own mechanisms for regulation at national level.
- Residential care for the elderly features widespread private-sector, some voluntary-sector and a declining amount of local authority provision.

We explored the perceptions of people involved in each sector of the strengths and weaknesses of different organisational forms and their suitability for delivery of the respective services. We discovered that many people found it difficult to make connections between organisational form and service effectiveness in the specific sectors in which they worked.

In the following three chapters we show how each sector and its organisational forms respond to the application of the analytical framework for assessing the suitability of organisational forms to the delivery of public services (see page 25). In each case, we consider whether these issues are relevant to the effectiveness of that particular type of public service.

4. Support services to schools

Current arrangements

There have been several developments in the management and delivery of support services to schools as a result of recent encouragement by the Department for Education and Skills (DfES). Some support services are traded directly with schools and some are centrally funded by local education authorities (LEAs). A DfES policy paper *The role of the Local Authority in School Education* (2000) contains the following proposal:

'*To help schools to be more effective purchasers of services, the Department is working on a pilot scheme in one Local Education Authority area which offers schools an independent "brokerage" service which puts them in touch with a range of suppliers and aims to achieve the best value from their delegated budgets. The service is designed to be funded by schools out of the savings generated by the broker. A number of such brokerage services could operate regionally or nationally, and the Department would be interested in working with other bodies developing this idea.*'

There is also direct encouragement of collaboration with the private and voluntary sectors and of cross-boundary co-operation between local authorities for both traded and non-traded services. The result has been several experiments and new initiatives in this area, sometimes directly inspired as a result of poor OfSTED inspection results of LEAs (OfSTED now has responsibility for inspecting LEA services). Key to the intention of this process is a desire to give schools more direct control over the way services are provided, and to introduce incentives to improve quality.

Experiments are most commonly with contracting out areas of local authority direct support services, including school admissions, welfare services, financial management, access and inclusion, exclusions, pupil referral, property services, information and communications technology, and services to governors. The experiments covered in this chapter typically involve some or all of these. In a few cases, new organisations are being formed to take over all of the functions formerly carried out by the local authority, including direct management of schools.

Service users in this case study are institutions (the schools), not individuals. The services provided are therefore at one remove from the individual consumer. This is a fundamental difference between service providers in this sector and those in the following case studies on social housing and residential care.

Strengths and weaknesses of current arrangements

There are several areas of dissatisfaction with traditional public service delivery in this area. Interviewees from local authorities and new contracting agencies report unclear targets and performance indicators, ineffective people management, perceived political interference obstructing efficient delivery, poor local authority management as a result of management posts in LEAs being held by staff with technical knowledge rather than management ability, problems with the recruitment and retention of staff, lack of investment and difficulty raising finance for major projects, risk aversion and a blame culture.

New contracted-out arrangements also have detractors. Persistent radical change creates fatigue and a sense of 'scratching round for solutions', and that contracted-out models are being tried 'simply because they are different'. There are concerns for staff who are 'TUPE'd repeatedly' – Transfer of Undertaking (Protection of Employment) Regulations 1981. It is also felt that once embarked upon this is a course that cannot be reversed, since the best talent is attracted by private-sector salaries the capacity of the public sector is thus further reduced.

1. Independence of government and political control

New service organisations report satisfaction with their arms-length relationship with local politicians, though the structure of contracts and targets means that their performance is subject to controls.

Authorities and contractors both have concerns about the perceived low level of skill in contracting on the part of local authorities. At the same time, both note advantages in distancing service provision from 'interference' by local politicians.

2. Public purpose

There is no national requirement that organisations delivering support services to schools should have a primary public purpose, nor that there should be any monitoring or regulation of this group for any of the support services listed above.

3. Non-profit-distributing organisations

There is no consistent pattern in this sector. Some support services are managed by trusts that do not distribute profit. Others are Public Limited companies (PLCs) with shareholders.

4. and 5. Preserving assets for the public interest, use and disposal of assets

The general pattern is for major assets to remain in the public sector – school buildings and other premises used for support services are not owned by the organisation providing the services where these have been contracted out. Thus this issue does not arise.

6. Public confidence

Local opposition to privatisation has been vocal in several cases. Local communities have feared reductions in standards, and failure to achieve targeted improvements in examination results in one contracted-out local authority has led to a penalty payment.

7. Governance and accountability

In the case of education services managed entirely by a not-for-profit trust, the board typically includes representation from local stakeholder groups, head teachers and sometimes central government interests. In other cases, accountability to service users is generally assumed to operate through the normal democratic processes of local government, and then through the operation of the contract for services with the deliverer. Deliverers in the private sector, where these are PLCs, see their primary accountability as being to their shareholders rather than to service users directly.

8. Finance

Organisations outside the public sector are able to raise finance outside public-sector borrowing, according to the requirements of their legal form.

9. Protection for users

Arrangements for the protection of users (in this case schools rather than pupils) are in accordance with the law as it applies to the organisational form of the entity providing the service. There is no specific protection in this sector.

10. Efficiency, innovation and enterprise

Some service deliverers see freedom from bureaucratic process and complex responsibility for a wide range of performance indicators as a direct source of improved motivation, since it is easier to be innovative and entrepreneurial when there is no surrounding set of bureaucratic restrictions.

Many of the new organisations have taken over former local authority staff under TUPE arrangements. They report that it is difficult to change cultures overnight, but that structure and culture changes are necessary, including increased clarity about targets, and that an entrepreneurial mindset has to be engendered.

In other local authorities the presence of potential competition from companies offering similar services is seen as a spur to performance, and as a barrier to complacency. Where LEAs offer some services to schools on a trading basis they may also welcome the recent arrival of competition as an incentive for their own improvement, particularly in cases where they are faced with competition for the first time.

Such outcomes have been positively received, with improved OfSTED results and apparent local authority and school satisfaction with the services being delivered. However, many of these arrangements are very recent and it may therefore be too early to judge them definitively.

Conclusions

There is little evident discussion of the need for new organisational forms in this sector. The key areas of debate are privatisation of services, conditions of service for staff and uncertainties about whether some private-sector operators are really in the business of service delivery 'for the long haul'. Some objectives in education are long-term and delivery requires long-term, consistent engagement.

The intention of many changes in this area has been, in part, to put schools in direct control of the support services they receive and to provide choice of supplier, and thus to stimulate competition. New delivery organisations most commonly take the form of companies limited by guarantee, though some call themselves 'not-for-profit trusts'. Ownership may be in private hands or with the LEA. Very few interviewees had given thought to whether these organisational forms were adequate for their purpose and seemed to be more concerned about services moving out of direct public-sector control.

There seems to be little debate about accountability to service users or to schools by deliverers in this sector. Although there is a general sense that accountability through public service contracting by LEAs is adequate, this may be because these arrangements are relatively new and there is little experience of the results to which the public can react.

Since many of these developments are very recent it may be too early to learn lessons from the different models in use. In particular, there is no established pattern of regulation for issues related to the contracted-out management of school services as there is in the provision of social housing, the subject of the next chapter.

5. Social housing

Current arrangements

Social housing, accommodation for people who would find it difficult to afford housing in the open market, is provided by local authorities and by housing associations. Most housing associations in England are Registered Social Landlords (RSLs). To become an RSL, an organisation has to register with the Housing Corporation. Most RSLs are, in terms of organisational form, Industrial and Provident Societies (I and Ps) for the benefit of the community. A smaller number are charitable companies; some are companies limited by guarantee. There are more than 2,000 RSLs in England, providing a total of almost 1.5 million homes.

RSLs in England are subject to the Housing Corporation's regime of inspection and regulation. (In April 2003, the Corporation's inspection role passes to the Audit Commission, where a unified housing inspectorate is being established to cover both local authority housing and RSLs.) The advantages of registration are that tenants gain the protection of Housing Corporation supervision and that RSLs are eligible to apply for the capital grants and funding that the Corporation administers. Registration is also very important in establishing the credibility of the RSL with private-sector lenders, and thus providing access to finance.

Local authority housing stock in many areas has been transferred out of local authority ownership to RSLs, and more of these transfers (large-scale voluntary stock transfers or LSVTs) are in the pipeline. In certain circumstances local authorities may also establish Arms Length Management Organisations (ALMOs) to manage their housing service. Transfer under an LSVT is either to a new RSL, created for the purpose, or to an existing one. Transfer out of the public sector provides access to sources of private-sector capital from which local authorities are excluded. This finance is increasingly necessary to meet the costs of repair and refurbishment of homes, costs that local authorities find themselves unable to afford, especially in the light of government requirements to meet new standards for the physical condition of social housing.

Strengths and weaknesses of current arrangements

1. Independence of government and political control

Neither government nor its agencies appoint the boards of RSLs and their finances do not appear on the government balance sheet. However, some commentators take the view that the independence of RSLs from central government is an illusion. RSL behaviour, some argue, is largely determined by the regulatory and financial regimes that are shaped by government. Others point out that the balance between independence and regulation is a matter of judgement about how to handle the tensions between the promotion of innovation and efficiency, the protection of the consumer interest, and the encouragement of the flow of private-sector investment. We explore these points further below.

2. The public purpose of RSLs

It is a requirement for registration with the Housing Corporation that the principal objective of an RSL must be to provide social rented housing. 'Principal objective' is taken by the Corporation to mean the majority of activities, as measured by turnover or capital. The Corporation also has to consent to any change in the RSL's objectives, before the Charities Commission will agree to changes for RSLs that come within its remit.

Thus, the public purpose of the RSL is ensured through the regulation process. Difficult issues may arise when an RSL wants to diversify into activities that may not be seen as mainstream social housing, as we discuss below.

3. Non-profit-distributing organisations

To register as RSLs, organisations have to be non-profit-distributing. Industrial and Provident Societies for the benefit of the community meet this requirement by dint of their organisational form. Registration as a charity also proscribes profit distribution. Companies limited by guarantee that become RSLs are required to have their non-profit-distributing status defined in their constitutions. All are required to use their profits to pursue their objectives, and any change has to be agreed by the Corporation.

4. Preserving assets for the public interest

The debate about the use of alternative organisational forms, including public interest companies, for public services has included discussion of whether there is already, or should be, a 'lock' on the organisation to prevent it changing itself into another type of organisation that does not provide public benefit.

In the social housing sector it is, in theory, possible for an RSL that is an I and P to take such a step. Although no RSL has yet done so, members of an I and P could vote to change the organisation into a profit-distributing company, thus ending the public benefit from assets that were, in the case of stock transfers, originally built up with public funding. Any RSL that took this route would cease to be one and thus lose the benefits associated with registration. The requirements for registration as an RSL are designed to create membership and voting arrangements to prevent changes in the constitution being promoted successfully by any single interest group.

The Housing Corporation has under review the possibility of an RSL converting itself into a profit-distributing company. In practice, if an RSL told the Corporation that it intended to change into a profit-distributing company, the Corporation's agreement would be necessary to allow the RSL to de-register and to grant the consents that would allow it to dispose of property.

A small minority of commentators are alert to the issue. Most people assume that the regulatory regime would prevent any such moves, which would, in any case, be extremely unlikely because they are contrary to the ethos, purpose and culture of the sector.

5. Use and disposal of assets

There are restrictions on the disposal of assets, intended to preserve them for the public interest. RSLs need the consent of the Housing Corporation before they can dispose of assets. Even if an RSL is removed from the register, consent is required, as we have seen, for the disposal of land that was owned at the time it was removed. There are exceptions under the provisions of 'Right to Buy' and 'Right to Acquire', which allow RSLs to dispose of homes to individuals for use as their principal dwelling. Revised regulations and guidance on disposals are expected in 2003.

6. Public confidence

Issues about public confidence in RSLs as a vehicle for social housing provision come to the fore when a local authority proposes a transfer of its housing stock. Tenants vote on whether or not the transfer should take place and a number of proposals have been rejected.

A majority vote for the status quo – to remain as local authority tenants – appears to happen for several reasons. Tenants are wary of a new landlord, an organisation that may be completely new and is almost certainly not known to them. The transfer is perceived and characterised by some tenants as privatisation, despite the non-profit-distributing status of the RSL. The democratic system that allows them to vote for or against local councillors is contrasted with the unfamiliar and, as will be explained in the next section, arguably less accountable board structure of an RSL.

Some local councillors are also resistant to the change, and to the loss of control of the housing stock, although transfer is intended to increase investment and raise housing standards.

7. Governance and accountability

The registration criteria for RSLs stipulate that at least one-third of the board members should be independent and that no one constituent group should hold more than one-third of the places. The Housing Corporation will also examine the constitution, voting and membership arrangements (such as the quorums required for voting in different circumstances) with a view to forestalling the predominance of any single interest group. In practice, some RSLs do have tenant majorities on the board.

Boards of RSLs established through the LSVT process are commonly made up of three groups: tenants selected from the membership of the organisation, which is open to all tenants on the purchase of a £1 share; local councillors or others nominated by the local authority; and independent members selected by the other board members. There are special arrangements with the Charities Commission for RSLs that are registered charities to have tenants as board members or trustees, since charities are not allowed to have direct beneficiaries in control of the organisation. An objective of this tripartite arrangement is to prevent the local authority exerting control over the RSL.

These arrangements for the governance of RSLs have been the subject of debate in the sector for some time, and it continues. Issues include the effectiveness of the tripartite boards, the size of boards, and the payment of board members. Consultation by the Housing Corporation on the issue of payment for board members, running until early 2003, is inviting views on a proposal that associations could pay board members up to £20,000 p.a., subject to certain criteria.

Some people argue that tenants and the local community should have greater control over the governance of the RSL; this would help to ensure that the organisation served community interests and was accountable to tenants and local people. The proposed model for the Community Housing Mutual, currently being developed in Wales, is based on these principles. A model constitution has been registered with the Financial Services Authority and is available for people setting up a structure to receive housing stock being transferred from a local authority. The Community Housing Mutual follows the tripartite board model, but tenants have control over the appointment of all members of the board. All tenants are invited to be members of the mutual. Tenant members then elect their board members from among themselves. The local authority nominates its candidates for the board; there is an option in the constitution for tenant members to choose from a list of candidates, by means of a vote. The third group of board members, the community members, are chosen to match skill requirements decided by the board. The tenants then have to confirm the appointment of these community board members.[6]

Within the debate about appropriate governance arrangements for RSLs, some people argue that as RSLs have become more complex businesses they require the focused attention of a small board of executive and non-executive directors, who could contribute more time to governance than current board members can. The arguments in favour of paying board members, who at present are unpaid, are based on the need to broaden the range of people who are able to provide the time and energy to participate in governance. In opposition to this, there is a strong body of opinion that paying board members would undermine their independence and altruism.

Some of the concerns about governance stem from a desire for greater local accountability. Many think that improved local accountability would act as a counterbalance to the current accountability to the Housing Corporation for standards and performance. Some people take the view that the regulatory regime has a tendency to create uniformity rather than responsiveness to local needs. They also maintain that it is easy within this regime, which is necessarily risk-averse, to focus on physical improvements to housing stock rather than on other important factors like neighbourhood regeneration and quality of life. This view is countered by those in RSLs who say that any such neglect is due to lack of resources, not lack of concern.

8. Finance

RSLs are estimated to receive about 50% of their capital investment from private lenders, who have invested about £20 billion in the sector since the introduction of private finance in 1989. Lenders are interested in the sector because of the fairly tight regulation by the Housing Corporation. The Corporation examines the accounts of RSLs to check that they are not overstretching themselves by borrowing more than they can afford. It is estimated that the role of the regulator brings the cost of borrowing for RSLs down by about 1% from the level at which it would otherwise be set.

Lenders require the security of that regime, especially as there is no profit motive or share price incentive to drive efficiency. They also recognise that they could not, in practice, take the hugely unpopular step of causing the eviction of tenants from an RSL that got into financial difficulty. This makes the role of the regulator particularly important in enabling access to private finance.

The pattern of lending has changed over time. In the early years of private-sector investment in social housing, lending was almost entirely mortgage-based. Increasingly, as the new assets transferring into the sector from local authorities are in poor condition and in areas of low-value housing, loans are being made on the basis of a fairly secure revenue stream

---

6. Ed Mayo and Henrietta Moore, eds, *Building the Mutual State* (London, New Economics Foundation and Mutuo, 2002).

in the form of rent and housing benefit. Some finance is obtained from the bond market, particularly from pension funds looking for regular sources of income.

Despite this diversification in forms of finance, the great majority of investment still comes from a small group of private-sector organisations. Lenders are reported as remaining somewhat nervous about investing in an area that seems so susceptible to changes in government policy. A few have withdrawn from the sector for this reason and because of the low profit margins.

Some people in the sector fear that any change in the landscape that affects funding could cause investment to dry up quite quickly. For example, the demand for housing, which, along with government revenue, gave lenders confidence, no longer seems so certain in all areas of the country. Government is also reducing the flexibility that RSLs have to raise rents.

9. Protection for tenants and lenders
The regulation and inspection regime for RSLs is designed to ensure standards for tenants and to protect them from the consequences of the RSL getting into financial difficulty. It also gives investors confidence. If an RSL does get into difficulties the Housing Corporation has powers to intervene and take steps to prevent its failure or bankruptcy. The Corporation can and does arrange for the replacement of boards. It can also arrange mergers and takeovers to protect tenants. In this case lenders will have a call on the assets of the failing organisation.

10. Efficiency, innovation and enterprise
There is some discussion in the sector about incentives to be efficient, especially with the absence of market forces in the form of mobile customers or the possibility of the organisation being subject to a hostile takeover. People who have confidence in market discipline as the only or main driver for efficiency inevitably see the sector as inefficient. Other people believe that efficiency is encouraged by several other factors.

The social purpose of the organisation is important, supported by the motivation of staff and board members to invest surplus in it. Regulation and inspection can help through benchmarking and the publication of comparative results. The Housing Corporation publishes details of RSL performance against a range of indicators. Further, there is the wish to reduce the cost of borrowing, an incentive that is strengthened by government control of rents.

RSLs are diversifying into areas outside social housing, including the provision of market-rent accommodation or accommodation for students. There are several reasons for this. Some make the case for activities that can cross-subsidise social housing and for economies of scale that can make the organisation stronger financially. Others suspect that the diversification is prompted by a desire for challenge and innovation for its own sake.

For organisations with a social purpose, diversification raises questions about the risks associated with developing new lines of activity. The Housing Corporation expects to be notified each time that an RSL reaches the point at which 5% or more of its turnover or capital is tied up with activities other than social housing, and at subsequent 5% thresholds. The Corporation asks for assurances that appropriate risk-management strategies are in place. Corporation policy provides for an in-depth review if diversification reaches one-third of turnover or capital.

Social housing assets may not be used as security for any borrowing for other activities, and the regulator will apply its policy to the group structure as a whole, as well as to the individual RSL. Despite these safeguards, there is some concern that organisational structures do not properly protect tenants or the RSL's assets from risks associated with diversification. Some people are concerned that if these relatively new issues were to be tested by a crisis legal opinion and lenders would take the view that it is not possible to insulate the social housing from risks taken by other parts of the organisation. For these reasons, a 'lock' on the assets might be an attractive safeguard, if it did not restrict the ability to raise capital.

Conclusions

Regulation of the social housing sector has the effect of making RSLs, which use various organisational forms, into something which comes close to meeting the criteria set out in the analytical framework developed in the course of this project, and which is very similar to the proposed outline of a Public Interest Company. As such, RSLs are a test bed for what might be achieved by such an organisational form in the delivery of services direct to the public. Although there is, of course, debate about the effectiveness of social housing provision, little of this seems to be about the characteristics of an RSL. The commentators involved in this study, who had a range of roles and perspectives, had very few concerns of a fundamental nature about the fitness of the RSL for its purpose.

The RSL diverges in one important respect from our analytical framework. There is no absolute 'lock' on assets or protection against certain types of RSL converting themselves into profit-distributing organisations in the future, although this loophole is currently being examined by the Housing Corporation. There are signs of an emerging concern in parts of the social housing sector about the security of assets for the public interest and their protection from risk. This indicates a need to investigate whether protection should be strengthened through the use of a lock on assets, as envisaged for a Public Interest Company, and what impact such a lock might have on access to private-sector finance. It is unclear at present whether a lock on assets would limit the extent to which they could be used as security for lenders and would discourage private-sector interest in financing the sector.

Regulation and the role of the regulator, the Housing Corporation, are responsible for shaping RSLs into organisations that closely resemble Public Interest Companies, which raises the issue of whether such an approach might be appropriate in other sectors. The implication is that the development of new organisational forms for public service delivery could be through regulation (and the legislation that underpins it) instead of or as well as through the creation of a new organisational form *per se*. Regulation seeks to manage tensions between various objectives – in this case, independence for the RSLs, the protection of tenants and the encouragement of private-sector finance. A similar approach to regulation may also be required in other areas of public service, especially where services are being transferred out of the public sector to independent organisations. We return to this issue in our conclusions at the end of this report.

6. Residential care

Current arrangements

Residential care places for the elderly are currently provided by local authorities, private care homes and voluntary organisations. The latest figures available show that at 31 March 2001 a total of 255,391 adults were supported by their local authority in staffed residential and nursing care homes, and 80% of these adults were over 65.[7] The majority of places, 141,245, are in independent residential care homes, which include some non-profit-distributing organisation (NPDO) homes but are predominantly private residential homes. This case study explores only the issues surrounding service provision in residential care, and does not include nursing care.

Residential care homes must now be registered with the National Care Standards Commission (NCSC), which also regulates them. Prior to April 2002 residential care homes were registered and regulated by individual local authorities. Homes must comply with the National Minimum Care Standards for Care Homes for Older People, first published in March 2001 and gradually being introduced. The financial viability standard came into effect in April 2002, and the environmental standards referred to in this case study, such as size of communal rooms, bedrooms and en suite facilities, were scheduled to be introduced in April 2007 for existing homes, but are now the subject of further consultation.

Private residential care places increased in the 1980s with the introduction of benefits for those entering private care, and to meet the demands of the growing number of people requiring residential care. Gradually, the number of private-sector places overtook the number of public-sector places, but the majority of places in the private sector remain publicly funded. Some local authorities have recently transferred residential care to NPDOs, either to existing ones or to new organisations specifically created to take over the running of homes. Other local authorities have already transferred services to alternative providers several years ago.

Potential residents seeking public funding are allowed to choose the home they will go into, which must be suitable for their needs and within the local authority weekly fee. Local authorities set the maximum weekly fee that they are prepared to pay. However, if a friend or relative is willing to 'top up' the

---

7. *Health and Personal Social Services Statistics, Table C7 Adults: Local authority supported residents in staffed residential and nursing care at 31 March* (London, Department of Health, 2001).

fee the local authority will usually pay its contribution to a more expensive home. Local authority homes must by law set a fee based on the costs of running the home. Private and voluntary homes set their own fees.

Residential care for an applicant must be deemed necessary under a care assessment before a local authority will contribute fees. Each local authority can set its own criteria for entitlement to a care home place. Once a person qualifies for a place they will have a financial assessment. The rules regarding payment are complex, but residents' contributions to fees are means-tested on both their capital and income, subject to nationally set financial limits.

There is much current debate about a crisis in residential care. More than 13,000 residential care places are reported to have been lost in the UK in 2001,[8] a trend that many believe will continue in the face of rising demand. Others maintain that there are enough residential places despite the decrease in numbers, because although we have an ageing population many more older people are now living independently, or semi-independently, reducing the need for residential care places. However, there is no doubt that residential homes have been closing in greater numbers than they have in the past. Commentators suggest that two of the main reasons for the high levels of closure are the shortfalls in local authority payments and the proposed introduction of environmental standards.

Strengths and weaknesses of the current system

1. Independence of government and political control
Private residential homes are ostensibly free of any government or political control, other than through regulation of standards. NPDOs are subject to the same regulation and are also free of control, but where they have been created following the transfer of local authority homes they may have an elected local authority member or an officer of the local authority on their governing body. However, most homes are so dependent on local authority contracts for care places that they may be strongly affected by local authority policy regarding residential care, particularly the level of fees paid.

Not everyone is convinced that being free from political control is desirable for the sector. There are concerns regarding the transfer of residential homes away from the control of local authorities. Even those who are not opposed to transfers *per se* do have worries about the move away from local authority provision. A recent case under the Human Rights Act has cast doubt on

---

8. 'Thousands of places lost in crisis-hit care homes', in *The Guardian*, 18 July 2002.
9. R v. The Leonard Cheshire Foundation and HM Attorney General ex parte; Heather; Ward; Callin [2002] EWCA Civ 366.
10. Donoghue v. Poplar Housing & Regeneration Community Association Ltd [2001] 3 WLR 183 (CA).

whether publicly funded places in non-public-sector homes are subject to the Act.[9] For example, there are concerns regarding the extent to which a home would need to consult residents if it were proposing closure. However, other cases regarding the block transfer of local authority housing stock to a housing association have found that in those circumstances the transferred tenants are subject to the Act.[10]

2. The public purpose of residential homes

Residential homes are not required to have any public purpose in order to register with the NCSC. NPDO residential homes may need to have a stated public purpose depending on their current form. If they are a charity, they will obviously need to have a charitable purpose. To be registered as an Industrial and Provident Society they must show that they exist for the benefit of the community, and that there are reasons why they should not register as a private company. For privately owned homes there is no requirement to have a formal public purpose in order to provide residential care.

3. Non-profit-distributing organisations

There is no requirement that private residential homes should not distribute profit. Clearly, owners expect to make a profit from their business. While NPDOs may not want to distribute profits, they do generally aim to make a surplus to plough back into improving their services. However, this may be very difficult for them given the current local authority fee levels, especially for organisations keen to provide quality services to publicly funded residents. (This is discussed in more detail on page 44.) One NPDO care home group reported that they have different fee levels for local authority-funded and private fee-paying residents. The private fees supplement the public ones, with the organisation's surplus coming entirely from the privately funded residents. Without the latter they would not be able to maintain the same quality of care or would become financially unviable. This raises ethical issues for an organisation that is intended to be for public benefit.

4. Preserving assets for the public interest

There is no requirement at present for any type of home to preserve assets for the public interest. So a residential home does not have to remain as such and could, for example, be sold to a property developer. However, preserving the assets, from the residents' viewpoint, may be of benefit only if it guarantees that they can continue to live in the same home.

5. Use and disposal of assets

Many privately owned homes are said to be struggling because of the low local authority fee levels, which have led to closures. This may be a particular problem where property values are high and owners wish to realise the value of their property. Low fee levels can also lead to closures in the NPDO sector. In April 2002, the Church of Scotland announced the closure of nine social care services, including five residential homes, because of the need to reduce the annual revenue deficit. The cost of subsidising care in the homes over the past 10 years had been £21 million. The Church of Scotland reported that it could no longer afford to subsidise what it describes as a 'public authority responsibility'.[11] A survey of 14 charities also reported that those organisations responding to the survey were subsidising residential care places by £11.8 million per year, despite regarding funding as entirely the responsibility of the state. Some homes had been forced to close.[12]

6. Public confidence

Public confidence in residential care is very low, particularly where local authorities have transferred provision into the independent sector. Few transfers appear to have been made without opposition, and some are the subject of ongoing objections. For example, notes to the 2000/2001 accounts of Sheffield City Council (the latest available) state that the transfer of its homes is subject to an objection by an elector who 'considers the transfer to be *ultra vires* and that it may be in contravention of the Competition Act 1998'.[13] Opponents argue that transfers are detrimental on some specific points, such as a probable deterioration in terms and conditions for staff, but often their arguments appear to be based on the political stance that provision of residential care is a local authority responsibility, and therefore should be provided only by the local authority directly.

The main protests against recent closures of care homes and against transfer plans have come from residents, their families and some sections of the media. The closure of care homes is so devastating for those involved, the opponents say, that many elderly people have their life expectancy greatly reduced by a forced move. Such distress is unlikely to be avoided by any change in organisational form, unless such a change can prevent all closures.

Even where transfers are to a NPDO organisation they are still described as being to the 'private' sector, and residents may feel they are going into the private sector when they and their families believe very strongly that the local authority should provide care directly. Those transferring to a different home may object even where it is of a better physical standard, since for many residents the 'best' home is where they live.

---

11. 'Kirk to close nine care services', *Church of Scotland Press Release*, 18 April 2002.
12. P. Burstow, *Cap in Hand: How Charities are bailing out the State in care homes for elderly people*, Liberal Democrat Party, 3 January 2002.
13. Sheffield City Council Statement of Accounts (2000/2001), Notes to the Consolidated Balance Sheet, 18, 'Challenge to the Accounts'.

If a local authority does transfer care provision to other organisations, it is likely that it will have to provide them with long-term contracts before they will enter into such partnerships and to enable them to raise finance, as described on page 44. This may create an added difficulty for potential residents, who could have their choice of home restricted if the local authority has guaranteed to fill a certain number of beds in a particular organisation.

7. Governance and accountability

The extent to which residents play a part in the governance of their home currently depends on the individual home, or on the larger organisation if the home is part of a group. While many make efforts to involve residents there is no requirement for them to do so. A different organisational structure could ensure such participation, and some in the sector would welcome a higher-level, and more meaningful, involvement of residents in governance, despite the obvious difficulties of dealing with very frail people. Other types of public service have faced and overcome the same problems.

Accountability for standards and quality has been since 1 April 2002 to the NCSC, which registers and regulates homes. The Commission for Social Care Inspection will take over registration and inspection from 2004. There is no longer a distinction between 'residential homes' and 'nursing homes'; all homes are 'care homes', but within that definition homes can register for different types of care. National minimum standards are now in place for all care homes, which must also pass a test of 'financial viability'. With the exception of some of the environmental standards, as discussed below, the national care standards and regulation by the Commission appear to be universally welcomed, and there were no calls for further regulation.

It is some of the environmental standards that have reportedly provoked closures. These are scheduled to come into force on 1 April 2007 and require the owners of existing homes that do not, for example, meet the prescribed minimum room sizes to undertake structural work to bring their homes up to standard. Some owners have decided that it will be too expensive to carry out the work and closed their homes. Local authorities that cannot afford the necessary upgrading have been prompted to look at innovative ways of providing residential care, such as transferring their homes to the NPDO sector.

In August 2002, following many protests, the Department of Health issued a consultation document proposing that existing homes be exempt from certain environmental standards and thereby removing the necessity for expensive structural work.[14] However, owners will have to state in their literature for potential residents that the home does not meet the minimum

---

14. *Care Homes for Older People and Younger Adults – Consultation Document* (London, Department of Health, August 2002).

standards. Although these proposals are only at consultation stage, many commentators are calling this a government U-turn. Responses to the new proposals have been mixed, but most people are of the view that minimum standards are needed and that removing the minimum standard requirement in order to prevent home closures is inappropriate. Others disagree and consider that the proposed introduction of environmental standards has already caused many homes to close needlessly.

8. Finance

Those who work in the sector report that the shortfall between local authority payments for individual residents and the actual cost of care is by far the most difficult aspect of providing a residential care service. Research published in June 2002 by the Joseph Rowntree Foundation (JRF) estimated the costs of operating an 'efficient, good quality care home meeting all national minimum standards' at £353 per resident per week for residential care. This estimate is £75–85 per week more than the average fees paid by local authorities.[15] Even if the 16% allowed by JRF for a return on capital for care home owners is deducted a shortfall remains.

In a recent development a private-sector provider of residential care complained to the Office of Fair Trading (OFT) that a local authority was abusing its dominant market position by purchasing residential care at unfairly low prices and on unfair terms, thereby contravening the Competition Act 1998. The OFT declined to investigate the complaint and in August 2002 the case was taken to the Competition Commission, which found that purchasing of residential care may be subject to the provisions of the Act.[16] The OFT has decided not to appeal the decision and will now reconsider the original complaint.[17]

While, in general, non-statutory-sector organisations may be able to raise capital to improve homes more easily than can local authorities, this may still be very difficult in the residential care sector. Some private homes, which have no statutory restrictions on raising capital, have not found ways to raise finance to improve homes, or, at least, have preferred to sell up. Some NPDO homes have also had difficulty in raising finance. The homes that seem best able to raise money are those that have long-term contracts for care, guaranteeing some income. They may also be the more established care home providers, and the larger organisations, which appear commonly as partners in local authority transfers.

---

15. W. Laing, *Calculating a Fair Price for Care: A toolkit for residential and nursing care costs* (York, Joseph Rowntree Foundation/Policy Press, 2001).

16. Competition Commission Appeals Tribunal Case No 1006/2/1/01 – Bettercare Group Limited (supported by The Registered Homes Confederation of Northern Ireland and Bedfordshire Care Group) v. The Director General of Fair Trading [2002] CAT 7.

17. 'OFT not to appeal BetterCare legal ruling', *Office of Fair Trading Press Release*, 2 September 2002.

Low levels of fee income remain a difficulty, with some commentators believing that, unless fee levels are raised, organisations providing residential care are going to find it hard to raise capital, particularly if they are new and have no proven financial track record. Some NPDOs have paid for improvements through existing surpluses built up over many years but building such a surplus may become increasingly difficult in this sector. Even if NPDOs can raise capital, servicing loans and providing a good quality of care on existing fee levels may be problematic, and almost impossible if they rely on local authority fees alone. But to rely also on private fees may bring the problems described above regarding the ethical issue of private fee-payers subsidising publicly funded residents.

Public documents proposing transfers out of a local authority often describe the financial or organisational arrangements only in vague terms. They may simply say the homes will 'transfer' in order to 'raise capital' but do not specify how this will be done. More specific details are available for particular examples, for instance where the local authority retains ownership of the homes but grants a five-year rent-free period to the new provider, or offers disused council land to an organisation in return for its taking over the homes.

9. Protection for residents

Most commentators seemed satisfied that the regulation and inspection of residential homes does provide sufficient protection for residents in terms of service quality. Where there appears to be little protection, as discussed above, is when a residential home is threatened with closure. A change of organisational form might provide protection if home closures could be prevented. But it is difficult to foresee a residential care sector where closures never occur, for example where demand for places in every home remains constant. Government backing might be required to prevent closures, which would undermine the autonomy of homes with new organisational forms. A more realistic form of protection could be to ensure that such homes must have strict timetables and guidelines for closure.

10. Efficiency, innovation and enterprise

Current local authority fee levels may make it very difficult for any residential care provider to be more efficient. Most service providers feel there is no scope for further efficiency without compromising the quality of services.

There seems to be little incentive for current providers of purely residential care services to innovate. Rather than do so, private service providers may leave the sector altogether. One residential home owner who had tried to diversify within the sector by providing day care services found that this was uneconomic because of the low fees paid for the services by the local authority. The sector is concerned with such a discrete service area that innovation and enterprise are difficult. Larger NPDOs may be more enterprising – for example, if they form part of a housing group they may be able to provide additional services such as support for older people to stay in their own homes – but it is difficult to envisage small organisations having the resources to do so, whatever their form.

Conclusions

The residential sector currently has several problems in delivering services, often related to the low fee levels they receive for residents who are funded by their local authority. Homes are said to be closing in both the private and NPDO sectors, as they have to run day-to-day services as well as modernise, using what they regard as inadequate local authority fees. Local authorities, which are also having difficulty improving standards in their homes, see transfer to the NPDO sector as an acceptable alternative to direct provision, because the opportunity to raise capital exists in that sector.

Many consider, however, that transfers to another sector, even to an NPDO, create difficulties rather than solve them. People find it hard to differentiate between for-profit organisations and NPDOs, and feel that the local authority should be responsible for direct provision of residential care. Ironically, local councils proposing transfers are criticised for an uncaring approach to people in residential care, yet those who accuse them wish residential care to stay under direct 'uncaring' local authority control.

A new organisational form, with a commitment to a public purpose and a 'lock' on assets, may be helpful to promote public confidence in the sector, if people can be persuaded that this is not a form of privatisation and that it will reinforce the rights of residents and offer protection against home closures. A new form might also offer opportunities for residents and their relatives to be involved in the governance of their home.

However, if local authority fees remain at current levels, organisations of any form may find it very difficult to raise capital. Only larger organisations with a long-term contract from the local authority may be viable, and these arrangements could restrict the choice of home for potential residents. The new national standards also introduce a test of 'financial viability', and it is unclear how this will affect homes outside the statutory sector, particularly those struggling to make even a small surplus.

7. Strengths and weaknesses

As the debate about organisational forms continues to develop, it is stimulated by various innovations and experiments. In this chapter we consider how some well-known examples of such innovation in public services fit with the analytical framework developed during this study to assess the suitability of organisational forms for public services (see page 25). We then summarise the extent to which the organisations in the three sectors considered here meet the needs of the analytical framework, before returning to our own original proposal for a Public Interest Company, which is also assessed against the framework.

Current and recent innovations

Foundation Hospitals

- The ideas underlying Foundation Hospitals were outlined in the NHS Plan in July 2000, which suggested that the best performing hospitals should be given greater autonomy from central control. This led eventually to the concept of their becoming Foundation Hospitals. Legislation to create these was signalled in the Queen's Speech in November 2002. The first will be operational by April 2004.
- Foundation Hospitals will be selected from existing three-star hospitals.
- Foundation Hospitals will be free-standing legal entities and will not be line-managed by the Department of Health. They will be held to account through the agreements and contracts they negotiate, through licence monitoring by the Independent Regulator and inspection by the Commission for Healthcare Audit and Inspection (CHAI). They will also be accountable through new governance arrangements involving the local community and other local stakeholders. They will have the right to borrow from the public and private sectors, but all borrowings will be treated as part of the Department of Health's budget.

The establishment of Foundation Hospitals addresses many of the issues raised in our research. However, there is widespread concern that introducing Foundation status for only the best performing hospitals may have adverse effects on other parts of the NHS which do not have the freedom, for example, to offer extra rewards and incentives to staff.

Controversy also centres on the decision to regard borrowings as part of the Department of Health's budget and thus part of the government 'balance sheet', as this may limit freedom of action.

Network Rail
- Network Rail is a 'public interest company limited by guarantee' (Secretary of State for Transport statement on Network Rail, 27 June 2002) with the principal purpose of acquiring and owning Railtrack PLC. It describes itself as a 'private company limited by guarantee' and defines a company limited by guarantee as 'not-for-dividend'.
- This new not-for-profit company has taken over responsibility for Britain's railways from Railtrack, the for-profit company with shareholders that was put into administration following financial difficulties.

While most have welcomed Network Rail as being a not-for-profit organisation it has been criticised on two counts:

- The Office for National Statistics (ONS) and the National Audit Office (NAO) apparently disagreed as to whether Network Rail should be classified as a public or a private company for the purposes of government accounting. However, in a joint statement issued in October 2002 the ONS and NAO stated that the different classifications were for different purposes, and therefore there was no disagreement. The ONS will classify Network Rail as a private, non-financial corporation in the National Accounts, since control of ongoing corporate policy at Network Rail lies with the board of directors and not with the government. Also, the Strategic Rail Authority (SRA) financial support facilities are contingent liabilities and not financial liabilities for the purposes of National Accounts. The ONS classification is in accordance with international statistical accounting manuals. Under accounting rules, for the purpose of auditing the financial accounts of the SRA (which is a non-departmental public body and therefore accountable to the Secretary of State) the NAO will account for Network Rail as a subsidiary of the SRA. Government interest in Network Rail is akin to an equity shareholder's interest, as it is acting as a lender of last resort in the event of financial difficulties. Also, the controls over Network Rail available to the SRA are consistent with a parent/subsidiary relationship as defined by accounting rules.
- The governance of the organisation has been criticised as having little true accountability, as directors of the organisation are accountable to the members of the organisation, but the members are effectively chosen by the directors. The SRA has the right to remove all members in the event of fundamental financial failure.

Greenwich Leisure Limited
- Greenwich Leisure Limited (GLL) is a staff-led 'Leisure Trust' structured as an Industrial and Provident Society for the benefit of the community. It manages 26 public leisure centres in partnership with four London boroughs.
- GLL originated in 1993 when the London Borough of Greenwich faced financial difficulties and cuts in leisure services. A local authority review suggested moving leisure services to a not-for-profit organisation. An independent organisation could benefit from government capital grants for sport not available to local authority providers, and tax advantages on business rates could lead to cost reductions.
- GLL has been successful in taking over the Greenwich leisure services and now also runs leisure services in the London boroughs of Waltham Forest, Merton and Newham, and in Epsom and Ewell. Since 1993 the costs of running the services have been more than halved. Turnover has increased from £2.5 million in 1993 to nearly £8 million in 2001.

Glas Cymru
- *Glas Cymru* is a not-for-profit company which took over the privatised Welsh Water in May 2001.
- It is a company limited by guarantee set up for the sole purpose of providing water services in Wales.
- Governance of the company is by a group of members who are selected from across the community.
- It is the first water company to move from an equity-funded model to a debt-funded model, raising £2 billion on the British and continental bond markets.
- In March 2002 the company announced profits of £24.1 million to be retained in the business for the benefit of consumers, and financial reserves of £241 million.

The three sectors considered by this study
Our studies of three different sectors – support services to schools, social housing and residential care – have illustrated how different organisational forms can influence the provision and delivery of public services. None of the three completely fits the analytical framework on page 25, although the Registered Social Landlord (RSL) is a close match.

The use of organisations outside the public sector for the provision of support services to education is very recent. Little if any thought has been given to organisational form. This is arguably less important when members of the public are not directly reliant on the quality and continuity of the service. However, an organisational form of the type outlined here could have a role to play in, for example, fostering greater confidence in accountability and value for money by local education authorities and among the public.

In social housing, the RSLs appear to be working well and meet nearly all the criteria for a generic organisational form for service provision direct to the public, as set out in the framework. This is achieved by a regulatory regime applied to existing non-profit-distributing organisational forms.

Residential care seems to be in something of a crisis, mainly due to the low level of fees paid by the public sector but also to the lack of protection for the public interest. There is a good case for a new organisational form to meet the needs of this service. Given an adequate level of fees, a new organisational form of the type outlined here could offer protection to residents and raise public confidence by helping to change the cultural expectation that there is no safe alternative to traditional public-sector provision of key services. As with RSLs, the role of the regulator would be important.

What is a Public Interest Company?

As we noted at the beginning of this report, the Public Management Foundation's interest in organisational form for public services was first signalled by the publication in 2001 of a proposal for a new legal form (see page 9). We described this as 'an idea in progress'; the current report further develops this idea.

In 2001 we suggested that a Public Interest Company would need to have nine key elements to deliver public services direct to the public. It should be:

- For specific public benefit
- For public benefit over time
- A trading enterprise
- Cost-efficient
- Entrepreneurial
- Securely non-profit-distributing
- Able to raise capital from the money markets
- Accountable
- Independent of direct political control.

In some of the more recent debates and discussions, the term 'Public Interest Company' has been used by some observers as a descriptor for a loose grouping of organisations delivering services outside the public sector on a not-for-profit basis. We use the phrase to describe *only* organisations which have all of the above elements.

The table on pages 52–7 compares the characteristics of the three sectors covered by this study with arrangements for Foundation Hospitals and Network Rail, and with our own model for the Public Interest Company.

Summary

Large- and small-scale experiments with new organisational forms are currently in evidence. In general, it appears that these were set up in order to address one or more of the issues highlighted in this report: for example, Foundation Hospitals were established in order to achieve a level of independence from political control and freedom to raise finance, Network Rail in response to the collapse of Railtrack and in order to avoid a conflict of public and shareholder interest, Greenwich Leisure Limited in order to stimulate entrepreneurialism and Glas Cymru in order to achieve freedom to raise funds privately while safeguarding the public interest.

Although each of these initiatives has focused on addressing specific problems in individual sectors, there is evidence that many of the issues covered in this report are relevant to all. It is important that lessons are learned from these experiments in order to inform future decisions about appropriate forms for public service delivery. There is nothing currently in existence that fully meets the criteria developed in the analytical framework.

	Support services to schools	**Social housing**	**Residential care**
Organisational forms in use	Various, including companies limited by guarantee and not-for-profit trusts.	Most are Industrial and Provident Societies for the benefit of the community. Some are companies limited by guarantee and registered charities.	Predominantly private sector. Some voluntary sector (mostly charities). Some direct provision by local authorities.
1. Independence from government and political control	Contracted organisations have 'arm's length' relationship with school or local education authority, but have to meet targets set in contract.	Independent organisations that appoint own boards. Government control by means of regulation by Housing Corporation.	Private- and voluntary-sector homes are independent. May have contracts with local authority. All subject to regulation by the National Care Standards Commission.
2. Public purpose	No requirement.	Registration as a Registered Social Landlord (with Housing Corporation) requires the principal objective to be provision of social rented housing. But see 4, Preserving assets.	No requirement.
3. Non-profit-distributing organisation	No requirement. Varies with organisational form of provider.	Ensured through regulation as an RSL.	No requirement. Varies with organisational form of provider.

Public Interest Company	Foundation Hospitals	Network Rail
Not yet established as a legal form.	A new form to be established in the current parliament. Local people, employees and other key stakeholders will be able to become members of, and therefore own, Foundation Hospitals.	Company limited by guarantee.
Key features include: 'an organisation independent of direct political control' – to be achieved by allowing Public Interest Companies to be autonomous bodies.	Foundation Hospitals will have considerable independence from political control. They will not be managed directly by the Department of Health and will be free-standing.	The board of Network Rail includes a non-executive director nominated by the Strategic Rail Authority (SRA). The SRA is a member of Network Rail, with certain membership rights, including the right to remove all other members (but not some only) in circumstances of fundamental financial failure. Government will effectively guarantee some of Network Rail's borrowings in the market, and the SRA is the provider of some finance. The Office for National Statistics (ONS) and the National Audit Office (NAO) take a different approach to classification. The ONS approach is that Network Rail will be classified as a private non-financial corporation in the UK National Accounts. The NAO will account for Network Rail as a subsidiary of the SRA (a non-departmental public body) when auditing the latter's financial accounts.
Key features include: 'an organisation for specific public benefit' (i.e. the intended public purpose must be approved and may not be changed) and 'a public-benefit organisation over time' (i.e. the purpose or form of the organisation may not be changed).	Foundation Hospitals will be licensed and regulated to provide health care and related services for the benefit of NHS patients and the community and to uphold the values of the NHS.	Network Rail operates under licence from the Department for Transport, which defines the scope of its activities. The Office of the Rail Regulator (ORR) ensures compliance with the licence.
Key features include: 'a secure not-for-profit organisation' (i.e. profit distribution would be disallowed, profits would be reinvested in the organisation).	Foundation Hospitals will not be profit-distributing. Operating surpluses will be retained only if used for the primary purpose of health-related activity in the public interest.	Network Rail is not able to distribute profits – this is prohibited in the company's Articles of Association. However, the members may change these in the future.

7. Strengths and weaknesses

	Support services to schools	Social housing	Residential care
4. Preserving assets	Not applicable to date. Physical assets not transferred.	Some commentators believe that it is possible, in theory, for members of RSLs that are I and P Societies to vote to become different types of organisation, with different purposes.	Numerous closures of private-sector homes and some closures in voluntary sector. Attributed to inadequac of payments from local authorities, and requirement to meet higher environmental standards.
5. Use and disposal of assets	See 4, Preserving assets.	Regulator's consent is required.	Private-sector providers free to act as they wish Charities have to pursue their registered objectives, but can close institutions.
6. Public confidence	Some vocal opposition to 'privatisation'.	Number of examples of local authority tenants rejecting transfer of housing stock to a RSL. Lack of confidence in a body not directly accountable to electorate.	Residents and relatives frequently oppose transfers from local authority to other sectors. Fear of closure of the home and objections to 'privatisation' and lack of democratic accountability
7. Governance and accountability	Varies with form. Some not-for-profit organisations include stakeholder representation on board. PLCs are accountable to shareholders. All accountable through contract with commissioner.	No one constituent group on board may hold a majority of places. RSLs also accountable to Housing Corporation for standards and financial viability. Debate about balance between accountability to national regulator and to local service users.	No requirement to involve residents or relatives. Regulation by the National Care Standards Commission

Public Interest Company	Foundation Hospitals	Network Rail
Key features include: 'a secure not-for-profit organisation' (i.e. profit distribution or making a profit through the sale of assets would be disallowed), and 'a public-benefit organisation over time', which might be understood to protect the assets in the public interest.	Foundation Hospitals will own their assets for use according to their designated purpose – this will be subject to a legal 'lock', preventing the sale, mortgage or use of assets for purposes against the public interest.	As a company limited by guarantee, Network Rail is able to dispose of its assets within the terms of its licence.
Key features include: 'a secure not-for-profit organisation', and 'a public-benefit organisation over time', which might be understood to protect the assets in the public interest.	See 4, Preserving assets.	Network Rail is able to use and dispose of its assets within the terms of its licence.
No examples in existence to measure public confidence; however the protections provided in the form might be expected to offer some expectation of public confidence.	As yet the public have had no opportunity to respond to the experience of using Foundation Hospitals as they have not been introduced. There is controversy about the wider impact of these on other NHS services, in particular that Foundation Hospitals will create a 'two-tier' NHS service with better quality services at Foundation Hospitals than at others.	Network Rail is relatively recent: public confidence in its predecessor, Railtrack, was low. As yet public opinion is not clear on Network Rail, though the fact that it is non-profit-distributing has been well received.
Key features include: 'an accountable organisation'.	Members of the Foundation Hospital will elect member representatives to the Board of Governors, which will be accountable to the members. There will also be a Management Board with non-executive directors. The relationship between the two Boards will be defined by each hospital's constitution, with some statutory duties for the Management Board to consult the Board of Governors. Foundation Hospitals will also be accountable through contracts with commissioners, through licence monitoring by the Independent Regulator and inspection by CHAI.	There are 115 members: • 30 industry members (the train and freight operating companies); • 33 public members (organisations, e.g. passenger groups); • 51 public members (individuals); and the SRA. All the public members are appointed by the board on the recommendation of a 'membership selection panel'. This panel is appointed by the board of directors. The composition of the first board of directors was ratified by the members in December 2002.

7. Strengths and weaknesses

	Support services to schools	Social housing	Residential care
8. Raising capital	Can raise capital from private sector outside the Public Sector Borrowing Requirement (PSBR).	RSLs raise capital from private sector, outside PSBR. Lender confidence comes from regulation of sector and secure income stream (rent and housing benefit).	Local authorities transfer homes for this reason. But many private- and voluntary-sector homes find it impossible or uneconomic to do so, on current levels of revenue.
9. User protection	Control of standards and quality depends on commissioning. Failure or bankruptcy of an organisation is possible.	Housing Corporation acts to replace board or arrange merger of RSL in difficulty. Thus tenants are protected from loss of home.	Regulation for standards. No protection against closure of home.
10. Efficiency, innovation and enterprise	Competition, real or potential, is seen as an incentive to efficiency. Culture change, when local authority staff are transferred, is slow and difficult.	No active competition for tenants. Some think this limits efficiency. Other incentives to efficiency include the need to reduce cost of borrowing, inspection, and publication of performance assessments. Diversification into related areas, e.g. student housing, is regulated to prevent exposure of social housing tenants to risk.	Shortage of residential care places. Providers say that inadequate fees for service mean that they cannot become more efficient. Providers see no incentives. More likely to move out of sector altogether.

Public Interest Company	Foundation Hospitals	Network Rail
Key features include: 'an organisation that can raise capital from the money markets' – it is intended that this should be outside the PSBR.	Finance can be raised in the public or private sectors based on financial performance and liabilities incurred, but borrowings will be treated as part of the Department of Health budget. The use of regulated assets as security for borrowing is prohibited.	Network Rail can borrow money on the private markets and is financed by payments from the rail operators. The SRA is also a provider of finance.
In the event of organisational failure, assets would be transferred to a similar organisation.	Performance will be overseen by an independent regulator.	Network Rail is regulated by the ORR and overseen by the SRA.
Key features include: 'a cost-efficient organisation' and 'an entrepreneurial organisation' – the products of freedom from political control and freedom to borrow.	Freedom from Whitehall control is expected and intended to provide opportunity to develop efficiency, innovation and enterprise.	As yet, the reputation of Network Rail in these areas is to be established. Some commentators have expressed concern that the complexity and size of its council may stifle innovation.

8. Conclusion

This study has revealed the complexity of the issues involved in relating organisational form to public service effectiveness. Such issues are not often discussed in any depth, especially amongst practitioners, and are not widely understood. It is also apparent that different facets of organisational form interact with each other and with their environment to influence the ways in which organisations work and what they deliver.

Many people involved in the day-to-day delivery of public services doubt whether organisational form is a real issue, but are very concerned about the degree of autonomy available to public service organisations. At the same time, politicians and policy-makers are proposing new organisational forms that offer elements of greater autonomy, and some of the other features that this study has identified as important. However, there is little evidence of any examination of how different features of organisational form interact with one another. This study has illustrated the complex ways in which they do. We believe that such considerations should be central to the continuing development of organisational forms for public services.

Such factors should also be a foundation for assessing the relationship between form and the specific purpose for which it is intended – the varying needs in different sectors or of different types of users, and the implications of the degree of direct public contact by various services. We regard these issues as critical. Experimentation with organisational form appears to address some but not all of the issues we discuss in this report. The full range of implications should be considered before change of form is undertaken since the issues are closely interrelated.

For these reasons, we dispute the use of the term 'Public Interest Company' to describe many new and some existing organisations, which differ from each other in important respects and not all of which share the features described in our earlier publications on this subject. In our view there are at present no true Public Interest Companies in existence delivering services to the public in the United Kingdom.

Financial freedom with the opportunity to raise capital is a major incentive in many new approaches to public service organisation. However, current discussion of concepts such as 'earned autonomy' for parts of public service seem to focus principally on specific areas of freedom (for example, freedom from areas of regulation and direct government control) while ignoring the need to be able to raise capital. We believe that the ability to raise capital outside the public sector borrowing regime is closely linked to the other objectives for new organisational forms and should not be excluded from their design.

It is clear that government and people working in the public sector could do much to address many of the problems identified by the participants in this study, *without* changing organisational forms. For example, the relationships between central government and local services, forms of accountability and the influences that shape motivation and values could all be improved.

However, we argue that there is also a strong case for experimenting with *new* forms of organisation. We base this on the evidence presented here that current forms can be limiting and that new ones have the potential to deliver services more effectively. Development and diversity will produce the learning that can help us to understand in more detail the relationships between form, purpose and effectiveness.

Further intellectual exploration without an empirical basis is likely to be of limited value. It is simply too difficult to discuss new solutions to problems when people's views are limited, by their experience, to existing solutions. We need to move the debate from theory and hypothesis to learning from practice. The range of possible experiment is very wide and opportunities abound at present – from small local social enterprises to large-scale institutions such as Foundation Hospitals.

Of course, diversity of organisational form, coupled with greater organisational autonomy, will inevitably lead to inequalities between the services provided by different organisations in different areas. Such inequalities exist now, but against the background of a drive towards standardisation and equity of provision. Best Value, for example, has done much to encourage standardisation and equity of provision in local government. Yet it has to be accepted that a corollary of more locally responsive services is difference in the ways in which services are provided, which may well result in greater *equalities* in the outcomes they produce.

This study has shown that two complex areas of performance by public service organisations require further development. These are the structures and processes of accountability for such organisations and the incentives that will motivate individuals and organisations to be innovative, responsive, entrepreneurial and efficient. The need for such development should not prevent the encouragement of diversity in organisational forms. These are persistently difficult issues for public services, and the public sector cannot claim to have fully effective models of accountability and governance or systems for motivation at present. Indeed, these were key problems identified with current ways of working.

The study has also emphasised the importance of the regulation of the new organisational forms. There is a need to continue to develop models of regulation that ensure propriety, standards of service and financial viability as well as providing a guarantee of public purpose and protection for users of vital services. There is a difficult balance to strike between autonomy and accountability for public purposes and public finance, and between the freedom to innovate and to respond to local needs and the protection of the public interest. This crucial area requires further exploration and debate – perhaps led by a consortium of institutions which currently have cross-sectoral responsibility for financial regulation, such as the Audit Commission, the Charities Commission and the Financial Services Authority. This matter is now urgent as new organisational forms begin to emerge in several sectors.

Recommendations

- Further research is required to explore new possibilities in greater depth. The cost of experimentation can be high for individual organisations, yet the testing of ideas in practice is important. We recommend that government establish a pump-priming fund to give financial support to organisations to explore and develop new ways of working with different organisational forms of public service.

- To accompany such an experiment there is a need for an independent body to monitor and evaluate the effectiveness of new organisational forms in practice, and to promote learning from previous experiments across sectors.

- Further research is required into governance issues in relation to organisations remote from direct political control. Research to be published in 2003 by the Office for Public Management shows that the governance of public services currently in the public sector can easily be diverted from focusing on strategy, to the detriment of the organisation and its services.

- Discussion is required amongst the bodies with influence and responsibility for regulation – including the Financial Services Authority, the Audit Commission, the Charities Commission and others – on the development of regulatory approaches that protect the public interest while encouraging enterprise and efficiency.

Appendix: Seminars held as part of the research for this report

This project included two seminars with invited audiences from public service management and policy and research backgrounds.

Seminar, 22 April 2002: Imaginative solution or red herring?

Nick Timmins of the *Financial Times* and Julian Le Grand from the London School of Economics led a lively discussion on whether the Public Interest Company (PIC) concept represents a real way forward for public services.

There was much discussion about the problems we need to solve – the need for greater efficiency, responsiveness, equity and quality – and divided views about the solutions and whether or not the PIC is a realistic option. What would be the motivator for PICs? Would this make them 'better' than what we have now?

Discussion also ranged across problems of governance and the difficulty of reconciling multiple stakeholder interests, particularly when the government has a key interest as primary funder. Another recurring theme was the possibility that a PIC might go bust. What happens in this case, if a public service has to be provided?

These issues revived memories of the experience of setting up NHS trusts in the 1990s, where independence from government was not achieved to anything like the extent that many had hoped.

The then forthcoming review of the voluntary sector by the Performance and Innovation Unit (*Private Action, Public Benefit*, 2002) influenced the debate: the current legal and formal framework of the sector is complex and some contributors felt that existing forms in the private and voluntary sectors can accommodate most initiatives; several examples were given. Others argued that there is insufficient protection of the public interest and of the way profits are used.

Many people saw the potential role of regulators in a PIC scenario as being crucial. The current over-regulation of the public sector would need to be replaced by a system that protects the public interest while at the same time recognising less direct control by government. Would this be possible?

The impact of and on the financial markets raised a further range of concerns about borrowing (as opposed to profit distribution) as a basis for financing.

Key questions emerging from the discussion:
- How can we be sure that organisational form has a direct impact on quality?
- How can customer interest be protected where profits are made?
- Do we really need new forms, or just a new approach to managing public services within existing forms?

Seminar, 25 September 2002: Governance and accountability

Professor Gerry Stoker of the University of Manchester addressed the seminar on accountability and governance issues. He questioned what accountability is for, and to whom services are accountable. He highlighted the importance of scrutiny, debate and sanctions as necessary parts of the stimulus for improvement, whatever the organisational form. He explored the role of governance and the access of stakeholders to organisations. He drew attention to tensions in both accountability and governance.

He considered whether a new organisational form such as the PIC could help accountability, suggesting that it could offer a focus for stakeholders to share accountability and to meet the various challenges connected with it, and could bring key players into a relationship with organisations. He considered the merits of two-tier boards as a means of involving stakeholders in a organisation without their becoming part of the management.

He cautioned against moving to new forms simply because of current frustrations, pointing out that new forms do not automatically bring new cultures, and suggesting that they may be more suitable for some purposes than others – for example, where there is little necessity to work closely with other public service providers. New forms could be counterproductive if organisations feel separate and different from other areas of public service.

The ensuing discussion ranged over issues of local accountability in relation to central government control and a culture of expecting change to be driven from the centre; the complexity of the governance challenge for lay people; and the importance of changing culture and power structures, which may be more pertinent than simply changing form. Many raised points about the changing nature of governor/executive relationships. Some questioners wondered whether new forms can really meet performance challenges.

There was support for the notion of plurality in organisational form as a route to reform in public services and away from the tradition of command and control. New organisational forms create novelty, which may of itself be a good thing.